Living On Purpose
With A Purpose

By Tia Ross

1

Table of Contents

Introduction

To the reader with a PURPOSE!

Though I came from humble beginnings, I decided at an early age not to allow my life circumstances to become a barrier for my success.

I have held positions with various organizations in which I helped to create, developed, designed, and supervise. My passion and dedication to see communities and families thrive allows me to catapult success and sustainability for those I serve. I have a personal understanding of what it takes to move through and overcome difficulties, as well as bringing profound level of sensitivity, compassion, and wisdom to my work. I am a Writer, a Dynamic Inspirational Speaker, and a Life Strategist Transition Coach!

As a result of my leadership I have been entrusted by Lisa Nichols, Founder and CEO of Motivating the Masses, to manage the youth and families' division – Motivating Teen Spirit. My Purpose as a Certified Master Facilitator and Director for Motivating Teen Spirit is to teach teens how to fall in love with themselves, communicate effectively, and make integrity-based decisions. My role includes training and supporting adults to facilitate the 'Safe Space' youth and family workshops; fundraising and management of the MTS Brand.

Through my purpose work, I have influenced the lives of thousands of teen and adults teaching them how to become influential leaders through integrity-based decision making, through effective communication, and community involvement.

At an early age I was determined to complete college despite my challenges of being a teen mother and living at the poverty level. I realized that my wealth would be up to me. With this desire for wealth and purpose I persuaded and completed my Bachelors of Arts degree in Criminal Justice at San Diego State University. My determination and hard work allowed me to create my life's journey of bringing others out of their circumstances. Through my leadership I have lead youth communities and families into emotional wealth. Under my leadership I have helped to touch the lives of over 220,000 youth and families. Motivating The Teen spirit has helped to prevent over 7,000 teen suicides and have reunited countless families. My purpose is to help youth and families to see their greatness.

Today I own a consulting company that provides strategic planning services for thought leaders, business owners, and communities. I co-own a company called Legacy Shifters designed to help individuals shift not just their own legacies but also the legacies of the people they touch through finance development and personal development. My journey on Purpose is not over! In fact, I am just beginning a new season with the launch of this book and a movement to bring people into their purpose so that our communities and people can become self-sufficient and change poverty! It is with Honor that I present to you a simple read for a complex topic in life. **Purpose!**

As you read you will hear some of my life's challenges and experiences that were designed specifically for you. I do not believe in coincidence. You are in my life for a purpose. I pray that this read will unlock your movement and get you into action around your purpose.

With Love and on purpose!

Finding My Purpose

As I write this, I know you may be thinking, "Here is a lady who has accomplished a lot. She knows who she is. She's got it all together. She has lived the journey and she has arrived." And yet, I know that my life is about continuing to live *on* purpose and *out* my purpose. I believe that life is a journey through which we live and grow; I am still on my purpose path in life and as you read through this simple but profound snapshot of experiences in my life and how they correlate to my purpose in life you will find some soul searching personal questions to answer.

Why Me God?

My anger toward God grew over the years as I watched everyone around me struggle to make ends meet, often time reducing themselves to the selling of drugs, sex, and their bare souls. Somehow, money was the common ground that connected the roots of evil in my community.

I remember sitting on my bed with my head down, tears of anger welling up and asking God: Why did you put me in this family? Why did you put me on earth only to struggle and be tempted to fall to the statistics that were predicted against me?

I vowed at the age of fourteen, to never fall into this trap of struggle. I was different! I would not be on welfare, drugs or the streets selling my body! I was mad at God, money and the adults around me who could not see that the way we were living was just plain out wrong! This feeling began to shape an unnoticeable bitter root that grew inside of me as the years passed. Somehow through the years of unwavering struggle, I became blinded to the truth of my real worth. Have you ever been caught in a habit; you know a daily routine of living? You start seeing tunnel vision and not seeing or recognizing what was going on around you.

That tunnel vision is what pushed me through high school, college and into my own business. I had blinded faith, not blind faith. I would state I am stepping out in faith! It sounded so good and made me look good too. More money was going out than I had coming in and suddenly an old feeling, lack of self-worth crept in as I watched one of my businesses fold to the lack of money. Once again no money and anger began to feel my heart. This time I was determined to figure this thing out.

How could I mean so much to God yet nothing here on earth? My answer was in the question. Thank God for the gentle yet sobering conviction of the Holy Spirit. I was measuring my worth by the standards of this earth. It was when I was again at my lowest point; no money in the bank, bills due, the place of struggle again that I realized nothing had changed yet everything had changed.

I could see how I had so much yet so little. I had grown spiritually closer to God, mature, and richer in my spirit, yet my bank account was again in the negative. Over the years God was depositing His riches in my struggle. I had realized that I had indeed broken every cycle and statistic that was set before me. I graduated high school, college and my neighbor-hood...without drug addiction, prostitution, or reliance on a gang.

Through the journey I was reminded of Jesus asking a man to give up his riches and follow Him. I had to ask myself: Is the one thing between my purpose and me my concept of riches?

The answer was yes. My worth was tied to the world's understanding and concept of wealth and I could not see how much I meant to Him.

It was the one thing that was in between my purpose and me.

What limiting belief have you made up from your childhood experiences? Could this belief be keeping you from living in your God given purpose?

Love Was In Me:

My life hasn't always been what you see today. I am half black and half Mexican. I grew up the older of two children raised by a single mom, living in the barrio and in the southeast ghettos of San Diego. From an early age I felt a big responsibility to help and support and care for my family and the people around me. I began working at fourteen years old to be able to contribute and have some of the extra things I wanted as a teenage girl. I wanted to feel special and needed. I was looking for attention and love. At the same time, I was looking for my purpose. I didn't see what I was looking for in the people around me so I went looking for love elsewhere, and in all the wrong places. I became a teen mom at sixteen years old. What often becomes a speed bump in the lives of others became fuel for mine. At that moment, holding my newborn baby, I made a vow that she was not going to live in the same environment. I was determined to give her more than I had growing up.

I was sweet and sixteen, and had it going on! I was the one that kept up with the latest hairstyles, Nike tennis shoes, and fashion. I grew up during the time when hot pink, neon green and big hoop earrings were sure to make me the popu- lar girl that all the boys wanted to date. Usually I would get my clothes ready the night before so that I would not have to rush to the bus in the morning. This morning however, I did not feel like doing all of that. I was so tired and really was not in the mood for dressing up. So, I threw on my sweats brushed my hair in a ponytail and hit the door for the walk to school.

I felt this way for a whole two weeks before someone no-ticed that I did not seem to be myself? I really did not give it any thought nor did I care. I stopped eating meat, doing my homework and just slept for most of the day once I got home from school. My mom would ask what is wrong with you? I knew underneath the surface of the question she already knew. "Nothing", I would say as I shrugged my shoulders and walked to my room to lie down. This same routine went on for three months, until one day when I was laying on my bed reading my history book; I felt the urge to throw up. My stomach felt really funny and my head began to spin out of control. What in the world was wrong with me? I was too afraid to find out, so I just ignored it and kept the same routine for next three months.

My mind could not help but to wonder if that day I snuck my boyfriend in my room was finally catching up to me. Could I be pregnant? My mom would always tell my sister and I, "If any of you "_____" come home pregnant you might as well move out and get your own place." She was not playing! So many thoughts ran through my head, what would I do, where would I go? How could I afford this? Would I have to stop going to school? How would my teachers and friends see me? Would my family disown me? Oh the shame that would enslave my emotions and cause me to give up. Would getting an abortion work? How would my boyfriend react? I was so confused and scared that I started to dress nice again, put a smile on my face to hide the worry, and get the attention off of me and I hoped that my thoughts were not true.

I was into the fourth month of hiding my worries and physical changes when I could feel something fluttering in my stomach that I had never felt before. This time it was different. This was weird, I had to tell someone. I called my grandmother and asked her if I could go with her to her next doctor's appointment to talk with her doctor about something. She did not mind at all; it was like she was waiting for me to ask her that. I went into his office, asked a few questions, and he decided to take "the test".

"Tia, the reason you have been feeling this way is because you are pregnant!" All of a sudden my heart dropped, I stopped breathing and began to cry out of confusion and worry. What was I going to do now? Abortion was not an option. She was already four and a half months old. For the next five months my family pulled together and began to prepare for the baby and I continued to feel God's hands knitting her together in my womb.

What do you feel you are lacking when it comes to your purpose? What are you searching for?

God's Plan For Me

My first step on this journey was to refuse government
assistance, which meant that I
had to work twice as hard. I had
a job and I was going to school.
I committed to going to summer
school so that during the school
year I could finish the school
day at an earlier time and have
the rest of my day available for
work hours. I was so determined
to make myself better and make
a better life for my daughter. I
graduated from high school at
seventeen and pushed on to college. I wanted to be a Criminal
Justice major because I knew
that I could change the environment where I was raised. I
knew that my street-smarts and

book-smarts would make me a great judge someday. I was pretty confident that I had it all figured out.

While I was in college I was offered a job as an intern to become what is was called a "coach" in the Juvenile Justice System. It was in that moment that my purpose began to really show itself. I began to see that God had been protecting me and pushing me in all the circumstances that I faced in my life. Before I finished college I already had a job and I was able to work right away within the Juvenile Justice System.

On my first day at work I was handed 14 files that represented several young girls who I know had faced some of the challenges I did in my neighbor-hood, teenage pregnancy, gangs, drugs, and criminal activity to survive. I will never forget that first file that I opened. The subject was a fourteen-year-old girl who was into prostitution. It was a horrendous situation but I knew deep down that I could help her. God had a plan. He had taken all those times that I cried my heart out and revealed the core of who I was and what my purpose was. All those experiences I lived had prepared me so that I was able to help that girl and all the other young people in those files I held in my hand weekly to review and create a plan for.

When you look back over some of the challenges you made it through in your past, do you see how you now

have the expertise to help others through theirs?

Finding Your Purpose: Worth

Throughout my life I've owned businesses and even built and operated a restaurant. I have gone to college, worked very hard, and experienced a lot in life. Throughout it all was a thread that pointed to a calling to teach the youth and people to use their hardships as a catalyst to live life on purpose. I wouldn't change a single step of my journey because I know that God had a hand in everything and there is nothing I would rather be doing than living the life I was supposed to live. That is what I want for you, as well.

The smell of making a dollar stretch to the next payday is like a pot of seasoned pinto beans simmering with salt pork in a crock-pot. I remember coming home from school and smelling the smell of slowly cooked pinto beans in the house. I would often help my grandmother clean the dry pinto beans as she prepared the oil and flour that would be used to make homemade tortillas for dinner. The beans would be eaten for dinner and then refried in the morning on the weekend with potatoes for breakfast. Yum, I never knew my grandmother was trying to stretch our food. I just thought we were eating really good food. Then she would say, "This is a poor Mexicans' dinner", as she placed the serving spoon in the beans.

All I know is that there is nothing like that smell of my grandmother's pinto beans.

I found it amazing, how the bean had no smell before it was cooked. The dry bean looked dull, had no smell and no one would every guess that it would be as tasty as it was. In fact, the way you know the beans were close to being done is; they would begin to smell up the house with an aroma of comfort. For years I helped my grandmother cook and stretch our food paycheck to paycheck. During those years God was teaching me the smell of faith. Faith is what keeps us going. We always knew that somehow God would supply our needs and make a way. As I grew into my motherhood I would often find myself preparing those same faith dinners for my family. As my daughters would come home from school and instantly know what was for dinner as the aroma filled the air, I would be reminded of myself at their age. By now I had watched God provide for my family year after year and my faith in Him grew stronger. He was always there helping my family through and making a way. I would have never guessed that all those years of making beans would pay off. I was about ten years into my marriage when my husband decided to go after his lifelong dream of owning a restaurant. Not just any restaurant!

He always wanted to own a Mexican restaurant in Atlanta, Georgia. This type of move would require me to dig into my faith like never before. Before you knew it, we were packing up our family and moving from California to Georgia. God was moving me to a foreign land. The seeds of faith that He had deposited into me had been cooked to perfection. I was ready to do this! After a long journey of uncalculated challenges and steadfast faith, the move was complete and the open sign was going up. Juan's Rolled Tacos was open for business! The smell of grandma's beans filled the air and comforted many of the customers who had made the same move from the west coast to the east coast; a familiar smell that bonded customers time after time. I remember looking at my husband

and saying, "Who would have ever thought that the same beans that my grandmother would cook to stretch a dollar, would be the same beans that would make a dollar. Wow, isn't God amazing!"

Divinely Orchestrated For A Purpose!

So how do you figure out your own purpose so you can live your life fully? How can you live your life without hesitations or limits? You were created for a divine purpose and the sooner you figure out what it is the better. But how do you do that? First you need to recognize your worth. Believe that you are not a mistake. Your worth is not your wealth.

Often we are taught that we need to go after a career based on wealth. What are we going to make from it? What money is going to come from it? That is the trap. Money doesn't lead to your purpose. It doesn't make you live life filled with passion. Money is simply a product of working.

We tend to put work and wealth together rather than realizing that worth is the product of your value. Wealth and worth are two separate things. Only God can put value on your worth. It needs to be tied directly to your purpose and to the fact that you are fulfilling the purpose for which He put you on this planet. From there you and God can determine that you do have worth.

Finding Your Purpose:
Experience

I remember sitting in the circle of women on a Monday night bible study class and thinking to myself: What do I have to offer to these women? They know more than me. I was in my early twenties when I was asked to be a Bible study leader. I completed the application process and answered average knowledge of the bible for question number 21. I had no idea what I had gotten myself into. I just knew it was something I had to do. I was a young mom, wife and in college, and now I had just taken on a ministry. At the time this was a five-year Bible study, focusing on different books of the Bible and I had started right in the middle of the life of Jesus. This week the lesson was on forgiving.

Each lesson consisted of about 20 questions and one challenge question. The point of the lesson was how God first forgave us and therefore we should forgive others. As I was preparing my lesson I got to the challenge question: Whom do you need to forgive in your life?

I thought to myself: I do not have anyone in my life that I need to forgive. I am complete with everyone. All of a sudden the Holy Spirit brought to my attention my stepfather. Out of nowhere I began to have all these emotions of hurt and shame pop up and I could barely finish writing my answers through the tears. I would think of the times I would wake up dreaming with fear that he would hit my mom again. I was the oldest of three and felt I had to hold it together and protect my brother and sister. I was all of 13 years old when the rage of domestic violence hit my house. I would take my brother and sister and put them in the room, close the door, swallow my fear and walk into the hallway hoping that it would not last too long or get any worse. I would grab the phone whenever I could and think: Should I call 911 or risk being in more trouble? Sometimes he would pull the cord out of the wall so I couldn't even think of calling for help.

I remember the last time it happened before my mother got up enough courage to bring in the law and have him removed from our lives for good. I was so full of hatred and anger that I had planned how I would kill him the next time he touched my mother. I knew I had the right to feel the way I did! All of these memories rushed my thoughts and I thought I had forgiven him by now. I began to realize that forgetting doesn't mean you forgive. The word said to forgive and forget, and I jumped right to the forgetting part because that was a chapter of my life that I wanted to throw away and never remember. I knew God was calling me to for-give this man who gave nothing but pain to my family. How could I truly lead this bible study lesson with this un-forgiveness in my heart without at least talking about it?

I realized the only way I could forgive him was to ask for God's help. I took the next month asking God daily to help me forgive the man who hurt us so badly. He began to heal my heart and gave me a heart of understanding and compassion for him. My forgiveness released him and me. Today he has a new family, is a pastor and keeps in touch with my family. My mother even talks to him to this day. I know God taught me how to forgive!

Is there someone in your life or a situation you need to forgive so that you can walk in your full purpose?

Experiences are necessary to growing your purpose. Look at the experiences you have had in your life because in the end, to live your life to the fullest, all you have is what you have been through - stripped down to the experiences that you have in life. I remember when we opened the restaurant and it failed. I remember the feeling of looking in our bank account and only having fourteen dollars and twenty-five cents. I had two house payments to settle each month and I struggled with my worth. It was in that moment that I realized that my worth, the money that was in my bank account was not my wealth. I realized in that moment that we had built an idea from a desire and a determination called

Faith! To be able to take an idea from a concept, to a plan and execute the plan to success was an amazing talent that came from within me and there was no way to place worth on that ability. The restaurant was a success and a learning lesson that got me even closer to my purpose. Needing help from others did not take away from any of the worth that I had in life. It did, however, help me have an experience that made me aware of how I can recognize my worth. Having that experience is what made me stronger and what made me able to tell you today that there is a necessity to recognize your worth.

True Joy is Purpose!

Ask yourself, what is one thing you would do regardless of cost? If there was no pay available for doing what you desired in the world and you were doing it just because it's what you love, what is that one thing you would do? Think about that for a minute. Explore it by looking back at your life and finding the common thread throughout your childhood. We were knitted together by God. Within the knitting is the thread that is our purpose in life.

Go all the way back when you were just a small child and think about something that you did effortlessly. Did people come to you asking for help or for answers to their questions? Were you a person's safe space in your family or at school? Or maybe you were the peacekeeper in your house. Maybe you were the person at school would stop a fight before it even started. You could have been aggressive, loud, outspoken, and bold - never holding anything back. Whatever specific qualities you had as a child is the key to finding your purpose.

I have traveled throughout communities and experienced different levels of poverty. I've been in front of some of the wealthiest people and in the richest places in the world. I've also been to the poorest communities on the planet. My love and passion to help people find their purpose is the mission of my life. I want that for you, too.

I can see the greatness in others and I can see your greatness. So ask yourself what your gift is. What do you naturally feel excited to do whenever you wake up? Is it to serve? Is it to be creative? Are you into technology? Are you naturally a very organized person? Or, is your life a chaotic mess because you are more focused on what your life has invested in rather than cleaning your house? The one thing in your life that has always made you stand out is your purpose. That is what makes you different. It's a jewel that's in our life and yet we are often discouraged from being different. We are encouraged to be the same. What I know at forty-two is that thing that makes me stand out is my purpose and that is what I was created to be. That's what makes me success-ful. I know that I am a super highly creative person and that makes me unique. Rather than trying to belong, and hide from ourselves, we can really truly find joy in our lives when we learn to live our purpose.

Finding Your Purpose: Possibilities

Once you have figured out your purpose, anything is possible. Lack of money has no bearing on your ability to live out your purpose. Your lack of resources will not get in the way if you make an effort to live your life to the maximum. I have found that God always unlocks resources on earth when we embrace our purpose and we live to fulfill that purpose. Say to yourself, "Now is my time to live my purpose." This is the best way you can live and truly enjoy life. When your wealth isn't tied to your purpose, then you'll find that you have true love and you are living a truly rich life.

What story are you trying to your personal wealth conversation?

Whatever dreams you have, whether it's to create a business, invent something, go to college, write a book practice medicine or become a lawyer - you have to pursue them. When you look around and you find that everything in your life is a mess, don't settle for what is around you. Go hard after your purpose. Live crazy all out for it. Live a life where you know that everything is possible when you live in your God-given purpose. As you do this, you will find that even strangers will walk into your life and ask how they can help.

I am not saying that if you live your life in your purpose

everything will be sunshine and roses. There will always be things to get in the way. You will always be tempted by distraction. We need to pay attention to the things that keep us busy and away from our purpose. Be careful not to spend too much time and invest too much of yourself helping everybody else rather than living the purpose that you are intended to live.

Distractions

Life is full of things that are fun, like watching TV, going to parties, or any way you can think of to have a good time. I love having fun. There is a time for fun and there is a time for discipline. Often times the subtle fun things have a way of getting in the way of living a purposeful life. There is nothing wrong with having fun, but don't let it get in the way of productivity. Don't look back and realize you wasted an entire year go by and you look back and realize you did nothing to improve or move forward on our dreams and passions. Sometimes distractions come in the form of small irritations through people or circumstances. Have you ever had a relationship that really stayed on your mind and took your energy throughout the day? I have gone through seasons of my life where I was in relationships that would stay on my mind and I would look up and half my day be gone thinking about what they said or how hurt and frustrated I was. I had to experiences that more than once before I realized it was time to live a life where I set healthy boundaries and did not allow anything or anyone to inhabit my time of day! I began to look at how many times throughout a day I was distracted by social media and conversations with people that were not productive or on purpose. I want you to really do an evaluation of what you are spending your time on through-out the day. Do an inventory of the things and people that you give your time to. Take a journal or use your phone to keep a quick record of what you do on the hour each day for a week. Once you have a snapshot of a full week I want you to group the times together and look at the hours of the day and the majority of the time in each group of what you did. Take that group of time or chunk of time and name it. Give it a label for example, Prayer and meditation, family time, cleaning up house preparing. If you come to a so-bering reality that a relationship or circumstance took up a lot of your brain thoughts and energy, I want you to STOP! Stop and Think and the Opportunity for

Purpose. The purpose of this distraction is to get our attention that there is something that has to be done about it, a healthy choice to accept your part in it and grow from it or the opportunity for you to release something that is holding you in a pattern of unhealthiness. When I look back at the things in my life that consumed me and were not productive I realize that I was in an unhealthy pattern and had to break it and raise my standard. Usually the breaking of the habit and releasing gave me a new lesson and wisdom to share with others because it did not get the best of me. It caused me to move closer to my purpose and live on purpose. Living on purpose requires intention and determination. A mind made up can accomplish anything. We need to be mindful of those things that keep us distracted. We cannot let those things control us or permanently distract us while we are trying to live our life of purpose.

We often take on other people's baggage as our own responsibility. I encourage you today to focus on yourself. Let other people's things go. Time can pass so quickly when we are focused on the wrong thing for such a long time until we suddenly look up and realize, "Why was that bothering me? Why have I given so much of myself to that thing?" I encourage you to get to that place where you can step away from those things in a quicker, cleaner fashion.

Self-Doubt

I was facilitating my sixtieth workshop for teens and families and my family was headed downhill. We needed to be sitting in my workshop participating in the very exercise that I was giving other families. I watched as breakthroughs happened, healing and love took place as frustration built in my heart. I felt horrible, guilty yet qualified to share my experiences with the families I was sent to serve. I was mad! How could I have such a calling on my life to heal teens and families and my family needed to be healed?

I needed a word from God. As I taught the lessons I could not help worrying of facing that heated conversation with my husband. He and our 16-year-old daughter were at it again. He had gone to one of his many extremes to get his point across and she had gone to the same extreme to get hers across. I felt so torn between being a mother protecting my child, to a wife who loved her husband. I just wanted it to be over.

This feeling of resentment grew over a four-year period. We were never on the same page with discipline and my daughter knew it. This was the strain on our marriage and I wanted out. I had been here too many times before and I was not willing to allow my husband to break her spirit. I continued to teach a lesson around family integrity and if my cell phone had been turned on it would have caused several interruptions. They just kept calling me and leaving messages that I just wanted to ignore so that I could stay in a space of focus for the families I was working with. The workshop was a hit but my plane ride home was not.

I cried the whole ride home...five and a half hours. I remember looking out the window at the clouds and asking God: If you want me to stay and not get a divorce I need to hear from you! I mean a miracle or a way so I know it is you! The only way that I will stay is if he agrees to get some counseling. We needed family counseling.

The plane landed. It was my husband coming to pick me up from the airport. He said with a confident voice, "We have a meeting with the family counselor on Tuesday." This was more than a huge step for my husband. He would not even entertain the thought of going to counseling or my workshops. I was over it but God was not.

Two weeks later upon return of another teen workshop I walked into a surprise birthday party. All of my family and friends were standing on both sides as I opened the door and the song began, "You Are the Source of my Strength", my daughters walking down the front door of my home with a basket of rose petals, the counselor waiting at the end surrounded by my favorite flowers...sunflowers.

John wanted to renew our

vows on my birthday. We restated vows. Then we reunited vows as a family in front of everyone. I saw my husband fight back the tears. God had finally spoken a word of life into my marriage and family. As I walked down the aisle in shock, the Holy Spirit gently reminded me of my request. He did.

Another thing that gets in our way of living our life of purpose is our own self-doubt: the things that we tell ourselves when we don't get the response we desired right away. We think that because we have talent, our purpose is going to naturally explode and we will make a difference and everyone will be the better for it. Often times when we don't get the reaction we expected we begin to second guess ourselves and shut down.

I have experienced this in my own life. One of my gifts is the ability to solve problems. I have a gift of discernment. I am able to see the big picture of things. However, some people couldn't understand it so they made opinions and stories about my gifts so that they could be comfortable with themselves. They called me "Sparkle" and "Hollywood." This is a gift of vision that not everyone can understand.

It's easy to fall into self-doubt and question your abilities. When I know that I am living from the core of who I am then I can go out and live my purpose and I don't have to doubt myself just because other people don't understand what I see.

There are things that you just know, but when you doubt yourself there is a piece of you that begins to die. The worst of it is later, when you didn't listen to that little voice inside of you, you turn around and say to yourself, "If I had only listened..." That is self-doubt and you need to step away from that so you can let your purpose serve the world.

What do you doubt about your purpose because you think you don't have it all together? Can you find your purpose in your perceived chaos?

EMBRACE YOUR IMAGINATION

I encourage you to dream big. Embrace your imagination. Think about why God gave us imagination. It isn't just for kids. Children naturally have imagination. Somehow through life we are conditioned to put aside our imaginations, as we grow older. I know that imagination is key to success in life. We can get distracted and stop dreaming, creating, and begin to doubt ourselves, but that will only lead us further away from our dream and purpose until what we know that we were meant to do seems impossible to achieve. You need to see the possibilities because imagination removes self-doubt and distractions. The only thing that exists on this planet is your imagination and the effort that you put into it.

Now is the Perfect Time

What I want you to do today to begin this process of living your life on purpose is to stop what you are doing and get in a quiet state. A state that feels good for you. Do a self-evaluation. Breathe. Reflect. What are the things that are creating stress and anxiety in your life? Where are you solid and grounded? Be honest with yourself. Be present.

There are a lot of distractions, but once you let go of them you can now ask yourself, what is your purpose? If you still don't know, then go back to the first thing we learned. Try and discover the purpose that you have in life. Once you find that out, ask yourself why you are not living it. Ask yourself if the things that are keeping you from living your purpose are still working for you. Sometimes we have gotten into such an un-healthy pattern that we trick ourselves into thinking that it is normal. Once our brain and identity becomes normal with it we then take it on as a living-breathing piece of us and we start to tell the story and live the story. Think about a time in your life where every time someone asked you what you were dealing with or what was going on in your life and you re-sponded right away with your overwhelming circumstance. Now, how long have you been telling that story or giving that response? Ask yourself what are you getting from it? Are you getting the excuse to say you are so occupied with it that you could not get to your real dreams and goals? Or are you using the excuse of Chaos to take the blame for your lack of success? Trust me when I tell you I have been stuck in this pattern and until you come to a resolve with realizing that it is no longer working for you then you will continue to hold on to it and get the same results. If not, now is the time to let them go. Whatever is keeping you from your purpose is a distraction and you need to let it go. It may be your lifestyle, it could be the effort you are putting into supporting others, and it could even be the excuses you make.

Now is the time to let it go. You may be a fifty-year-old, 30-year-old, or even 20; there is no age in time when it comes to purpose. Now is always the perfect time to live on purpose. It will always be the perfect time. So what is keeping you from living the life that God intended for you? In the end, a life on purpose requires a made up mind. Literally anything is available to you and nothing is out of reach. No one and nothing can get in the way of you living your life the way you should. Make up your mind that you are now going to live YOU on purpose with a purpose!

Made in the USA
Columbia, SC
10 June 2018